Public Speaking
for Wimps

Public Speaking

for
Wimps

Staying Cool When Stage Fright Strikes

Rich Mintzer

Photography by Peter Murdock

STERLING PUBLISHING CO., INC.
NEW YORK

Design by Lubosh Cech *okodesignstudio.com*
Photography by Peter Murdock

Models: David Barkhymer; Jay Gaussoin; Pamela Martin; Joe Mode; Gilberto Moreno;
Holly Teichholtz; Adrienne Truscott; Gina Vetro; Scott Vinnacombe; Matthew Wittmeyer

Library of Congress Cataloging-in-Publication Data

Mintzer, Richard.
  Public speaking for wimps; staying cool when stage fright strikes / Rich Mintzer;
photography by Peter Murdock.
      p. cm.
  Includes index.
  ISBN 1-4027-1224-3
  1. Public speaking. 2. Stage fright. I. Title.

PN4129.15.M56 2005
808.5'1—dc22

                                        2005001297

10 9 8 7 6 5 4 3 2 1

Published by Sterling Publishing Co., Inc.
387 Park Avenue South, New York, NY 10016
© 2005 Rich Mintzer
Distributed in Canada by Sterling Publishing
c/o Canadian Manda Group, 165 Dufferin Street
Toronto, Ontario, Canada M6K 3H6
Distributed in Great Britain by Chrysalis Books Group PLC
The Chrysalis Building, Bramley Road, London W10 6SP, England
Distributed in Australia by Capricorn Link (Australia) Pty. Ltd.
PO Box 704, Windsor, NSW 2756, Australia

Sterling ISBN 1-4027-1224-3

For information about custom editions, special sales, premium and
corporate purchases, please contact Sterling Special Sales
Department at 800-805-5489 or specialsales@sterlingpub.com.

Acknowledgments

I'd like to thank Danielle Truscott for the opportunity to write this book. It's been great fun.

I'd also like to thank the public speakers whom I've come in contact with prior to and while writing *Public Speaking for Wimps.* Watching, listening to, and learning from many different types of speakers and performers, including both professionals and former wimps like me, have provided me with a greater understanding of what it takes to speak in front of other people. From Les Brown and Tony Roberts to Bill Clinton and Bill Cosby there is something to be learned from the manner in which they draw in an audience and hold them. I've also learned a great deal from my friends, colleagues, students, and associates, and I thank them for allowing me to gain insights—many of which were unintended—into the manner in which people approach and deliver material in a public setting.

On a personal note, I'd like to thank several of my communications professors and, as always, my family, who are supportive and try to keep the TV volume turned down while I'm writing another book. Watching my daughter, Rebecca, sing and my son, Eric, tell jokes in their grade-school talent show was both heartwarming and encouraging. I hope they never lose the confidence to get up and speak or perform in front of others.

Contents

Preface **9**

Why Is Everyone So Nervous About Public Speaking? **12**

Getting Started **16**

Instant Public Speaking: Ready, Get Set, Go! **20**

Basic Relaxation Exercises **22**

Relaxing Before You Speak **26**

Visualization **30**

Planning and Preparation **32**

Practice, Practice, Practice **40**

Suggestions for Instant Public Speaking **51**

Fix-Its **52**

Fear Factor: Stage Fright **54**

Jump-starting Your Speech or Presentation **56**

Fixing Foul-Ups: Can We Start This Over? **57**

Beating the First-Impression Blues **58**

Memory Mending **60**

Mastering the Microphone **62**

Fashion Fix-Its: Dressing for Success **66**

A Priest, a Rabbi, and a Minister, or How to Use Appropriate Humor **68**

At a Loss for Words **70**

Better Posture and Personality **74**

Props: Know When to Hold Them and When to Fold Them **78**

Oh No, I Can't Stop Talking: The Use of Pauses **80**

Now Say It with Feeling **81**

Loosening Up: Adding Some Movement **82**

Call to Arms: What to Do with Those Hands and Arms **84**

Is Your Body Talking Too Much? Body Language **88**

Qualms with Questions **90**

Better Introductions **91**

Keeping Them Awake **92**

Last-Second Checklist **93**

Many Types of Presentations: Putting It All Together **94**

The Acceptance Speech **96**

The Panelist **98**

The Toast **99**

The Sales Pitch: Persuasive Speaking **100**

The Roast **102**

As Master of Ceremonies **104**

The Rebuttal or Response **106**

Welcoming Speeches **108**

Paying Tribute **109**

Mastering the Meeting **110**

Up in Front of the Class: The Informative Speech **112**

Mastering Television **114**

You've Got the Perfect Look for Radio **116**

When They Call On You: Impromptu Speaking **118**

High Drama: Onstage Performances **120**

A Final Word **122**

About the Models **124**

Index **126**

Preface

It's almost unavoidable! No matter how hard you try, at some time you will find yourself in a situation in which you will have to speak in public. For some of us, this is an opportunity to step up and deliver a message with poise and confidence. However, for most of us, this is an anxiety-provoking experience, one akin to hiking across very rough, mountainous terrain. We immediately envision ourselves proceeding with great caution, stumbling over words, tripping over sentences and falling over paragraphs. Many a first-time public speaker would opt to climb Mount Everest or bungee-jump from the Golden Gate Bridge rather than speak in front of other people.

To say "I can do it" as you are approaching the podium is hardly reassuring, since your sweaty palms, shaky knees, and dry mouth beg to differ. However, it simply cannot be as hard as it seems. After all, lecturers, renowned spokespersons, and former politicians have made very significant sums of money touring the country pontificating to large crowds. In addition, there are speaker's bureaus ready to hawk tapes and sell you books designed to make you one of those marketable motivational speakers jetting around the country on the professional speaking circuit. Making the rounds on the professional speaking circuit is not a realistic goal for most people, myself included. However, being able to get up and speak in public with confidence and inner calm is something you can achieve, as I have.

Whether it's a speech at the local PTA meeting, a toast at a wedding, a pep talk to your softball team, a graduation speech at your alma mater, a training session for new employees, or a major marketing presentation before the board of directors, every public speaking opportunity will have one thing in common: the need to convey a message clearly to an audience (ideally with some pizzazz).

Public Speaking for Wimps is a user-friendly guide to becoming a more polished speaker in any public setting. It is not designed to make you the next Winston Churchill (though if it does, I'd love to hear from you). Rather, this book will offer a non-threatening, nonanalytical, straightforward, and entertaining approach to speaking in front of three or three thousand people.

Within these pages you'll find tips on how to organize and plan ahead, methods of relaxation, how to practice, injecting appropriate humor, tailoring your speech to meet the needs of an audience, making eye contact, and even using gestures and body language.

If I Did It, Anyone Can

As a child I was very shy. Even into my twenties, the thought of speaking in front of people made me very nervous. The rare occasion on which I was asked to speak in front of an assembly or an audience of any type left me feeling nervous and unsure of myself. I would write out my words very carefully, always opting for the shortest possible speech, and then mechanically make my way through my script.

After graduating from college, I pursued a writing career. By some twist of fate I was asked to write for comedians appearing in the Poconos and Catskills. As I wrote their comedy routines and watched them perform, I began to picture myself standing up there and delivering a routine. I found it amazing how individuals who certainly wouldn't consider themselves brave weren't fazed by speaking in front of a roomful of people. In fact, they were putting themselves right out there on the line, trying to make people laugh. One comic I wrote for had a fear of tunnels, flying, heights, elevators, and numerous other things, yet somehow she thought nothing of going onstage in a packed comedy club and trying to be funny.

So, after writing for numerous stand-up comics and watching several of them butcher my material, I decided that if they could go onstage, I could too. So one Sunday night I stepped onto the stage of Dangerfield's night club in front of a scattered few customers and many empty seats. Of course I didn't do very well, but to my surprise I didn't feel all that scared. Like Rodney himself, I got no respect, but I did survive up there. I had taken to speaking in public, and in one of the toughest possible forums to boot: stand-up comedy.

In the beginning I crafted my words very carefully. With time and practice, however, my words began to sound less scripted and more off the cuff, and I noticed that I was getting bigger laughs. This made me feel more confident onstage, and I began to ad-lib as necessary. One night I followed a foul-mouthed young would-be comic whose marginally funny material was overwhelmed by the use of four-letter words. Walking onto the stage, I thanked the comic for performing, then remarked to the crowd, "She's available for weddings, bar mitzvahs, and kids' parties." It broke the tension she had created, and it also got a big laugh. And it made me realize I could think on my feet.

In time I found myself co-hosting a radio show and exploring other forms of speaking, such as seminars. I also began to study what it was that made a speaker successful. Why did one speaker connect with an audience while another bombed? What made for an effective presentation? How come certain speakers could easily replace sleeping pills? Studying speakers and the reactions of their audiences gave me many of the answers. They were, in fact, rather simple. Public speaking was not rocket science. It simply employed many fundamentals of communications, some of which I'd learned as a communications major in college. It also employed aspects of psychology, my minor in college and postgraduate field of study. I realized three things:

1. Public speaking means connecting with your audience and delivering a message.

2. The fear of public speaking is primarily psychological.

3. My parents hadn't completely wasted their money sending me to school.

After my wife and I adopted our daughter in 1992, we became very involved in the adoption arena, and eventually I found myself doing lectures, workshops, and presentations about adoption and even hosting a radio show on the subject. My knowledge of the subject matter and my comfort speaking in public made these speaking engagements enjoyable— and, from what I've been told, very helpful to those in attendance.

I decided to write this book to help make the transition from sweaty palms and shyness to comfortable public speaking easier for anyone who has ever stepped up to the microphone and heard her heart beating louder than her voice. No, I'm not a polished, nationally touring motivational speaker and probably never will be. I am, however, someone who was once scared of public speaking (a wimp) but now looks forward to chairing meetings, giving lectures, and appearing at other speaking engagements.

Why Is Everyone
So Nervous

About Public Speaking?

Let's face it—if you're going to stand up and speak in front of a roomful of people, you should be nervous. If you're not, it means you're either a very savvy public speaker, not fully aware of the speaking situation, or drunk.

So why does the mere thought of speaking in public make so many of us queasy?

It's human nature to want to make a positive impression on other people. People go to great lengths to make a good impression on others, from taking classes in speech, etiquette, and presentation skills to shopping for the right outfits and even undergoing plastic surgery. Billions of dollars are spent every year on products and services to help us look and sound better in front of our peers. And to make matters worse, television has raised the bar by featuring attractive people who sound remarkably at ease in front of the camera. Now all of us are that much more conscious of how we appear in front of others.

Speaking in public accentuates those feelings of wanting to make a good impression. We feel our own insecurities being magnified, and we are keenly aware of being judged. In addition, we want to sound intelligent, poised, and professional—we definitely don't want to make fools of ourselves. With all of that at stake, it's no wonder we are so frightened of speaking in public.

And yet every day millions of people get up and speak in front of others. How is that possible if we have so much to lose? Very simple—change your mind-set.

Okay, that's easier said than done. Nonetheless, if you change your attitude from "What if I make a fool of myself?" to "What if I really wow them?" you're already on the right path to a more positive mind-set. It's amazing how many people will dwell on the potential negative scenarios in contrast to how few will visualize people walking up to them after their speech or presentation and saying, "Nice job" or "I really enjoyed your talk." The thought of impending disaster overshadows the potential positive feeling of a job well done. If a baseball player visualized striking out more often than rounding the bases, he probably never would have stuck with the sport. So why not put the same positive imagery to work for yourself?

If you stop and think about it, you'll probably find that 99 percent of the public speaking engagements that you have been a witness to in the past six months have gone just fine. The question isn't whether the speakers were great orators but simply how many met with disaster? For the vast majority of speakers, their clothes didn't suddenly fall off, pigeons didn't swoop down and take away their notes, and they didn't forget their speech (and even if a speaker missed a line or two, or ten, you

didn't even know it). It's likely that you cannot remember a real public speaking disaster that you have witnessed in recent memory.

The key to successful public speaking is preparation. If you are confident that you know your material and can explain it clearly to the mirror or to a friend or colleague, then most likely you are ready to speak. At that point the number of people watching or listening should not matter. Your presentation is ready, and you're ready. The audience will enjoy, appreciate, be entertained by, or be educated by what you have to say. And, if not, that's no longer your concern— you've done your part. You cannot control your surroundings, but once you are well prepared and rehearsed, you *can* get up there and speak with confidence.

We tend to think that the audience is 100 percent focused on how we look and what we have to say. Sorry, but unless you're giving the State of the Union address or presenting at the Academy Awards, all eyes and ears typically do not remain on you as you speak. In fact, surveys have shown that audience members typically remember very little of a speech or presentation, even a short one. At least a few of the people in the front rows have to go to the restroom and are wondering how they can get out without being noticed. A good number of the people in the middle rows are half listening and half daydreaming, while the people in the back rows can't see you very well and are covertly studying the people in the seats around them. In short, no one is 100 percent focused on you. If, in fact, you do so well up there as to make them forget their other concerns, then you have succeeded beyond your wildest hopes. If not, you've simply succeeded in delivering your message.

The old saying "You are your own worst critic" is especially apropos when it comes to public speaking. It is primarily what is going on in our own minds that makes us so nervous about speaking in public.

Many famous speakers and performers had stage fright, from Winston Churchill to Carly Simon. Yet they rose to the occasion and channeled that fear in a way that helped them give a stellar speech or performance. You can channel your nervous energy through positive imagery and think, "I'm going to wow them."

Getting Started

It's been said that the only thing scarier than death is speaking in public. It doesn't have to be that way. Public Speaking for Wimps *is designed to provide the basic information necessary for you to feel more confident and comfortable in public speaking situations. The goal of this book is to help you conquer fear by first learning how to relax, prepare, and practice.*

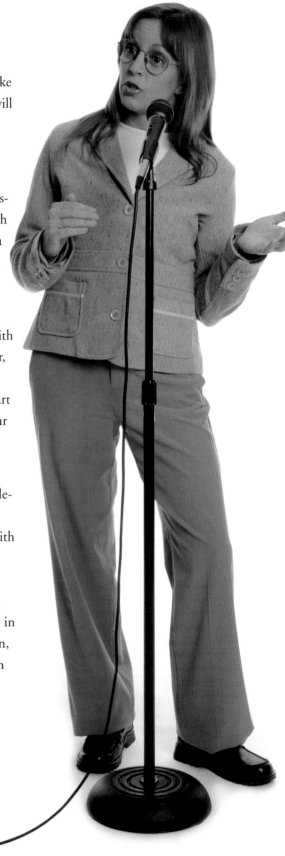

You've probably heard it many times before, but the suggestion that you should picture the audience naked does have some merit. You're standing vulnerable before them—feeling naked, in a way—so imagining them literally naked can make things feel a little more equal. True confidence, however, comes not from how you picture them but from how much you believe yourself, what you have to say, and how you present it. (Okay, sometimes picturing them naked is fun, too.)

To get you started, the next several pages present some exercises and techniques to help you relax, prepare, and practice.

Relaxation will help you eliminate negative energy and open the door to positive visualization and positive energy. Instead of harboring stress, your mind and body will focus at the task at hand: communicating.

Preparation is the cornerstone to speaking success. Researching,

planning and organizing will make your job that much easier. You will have more confidence if you are properly prepared to speak.

Practice may not make perfect, but it will help you eliminate mistakes and familiarize yourself with the material. It will also help you hone your communication skills. Practice also provides a time to experiment.

No, it won't all come together with one session in front of the mirror, but in time, using some or all of the techniques listed, you can start the process that will improve your public speaking abilities.

The type of speaking you are preparing to do is somewhat irrelevant at the initial practice stage. Later you will hone your skills with more specific types of speaking engagements in mind. For now, you just want to get comfortable with the general idea of speaking in front of other people—being seen, being heard, and connecting with your audience.

A VERY IMPORTANT STEP

First and foremost, you need to tell yourself, possibly even out loud:

There is no reason to fear public speaking, none whatsoever.

People speak in public every day—in front of business colleagues, friends, family members and large audiences of strangers. They do it, they survive, and more often than not they feel very good about having spoken.

WHERE TO START

A quiet, relaxing place, with minimal distractions, will allow you to focus on the initial relaxation and breathing exercises. It will also allow you to close your eyes and visualize, as well as to gather your thoughts as you structure and build your presentation. Try your office, the den at home, or even the public library.

After you have been practicing for a while, you'll want to find a place where you can set up a video camera to tape yourself. Later, shift to a noisier place, since there are usually distractions around you when you speak in a public setting. Finally, look for someplace that resembles the setting in which you will be speaking.

A FEW THINGS TO ALWAYS REMEMBER

As you embark on the road to more comfortable, polished public speaking, you should take with you ten tidbits that will serve you well.

1. If you're worried about speaking in public, know that you're not alone.

2. You don't appear as nervous as you think you do—most people can't even tell.

3. The audience is usually on your side. They want you to succeed.

4. It's okay to express vulnerability—in fact, it's typically well received.

5. You don't have to be perfect. If you mess up or make a mistake, just keep on going.

6. Set aside time to prepare.

7. Set aside time to practice.

8. Don't forget to breathe when you speak.

9. Remember to make eye contact with your audience.

10. Try to have fun up there!

Remember, most of us are wimps when it comes to public speaking, just trying not to fall on our faces. With that in mind, I invite all of you to muster up your energy and, as the sneaker giant says, just do it. Once you step away from the microphone and just one person walks up to you afterward and tells you that he or she benefited from what you had to say, you'll no longer feel like a wimp—you'll feel like a great orator.

Instant Public Speaking:

Ready, Get Set, Go!

Included in this section are some simple relaxation and visualization exercises followed by simple techniques of preparing and rehearsing. Each segment is designed to help get you started on the road to successful public speaking. In the last section I'll give you a few suggestions for places where you can try instant public speaking—that is, where you can gain experience presenting your ideas in public without all the pressure that comes with a formal speaking engagement.

Basic Relaxation Exercises

Relaxation exercises come in handy whenever you feel stress about speaking in public, whether you are preparing to speak in a month or going onstage that evening. The following sequence of relaxation exercises is a simple way to calm your nerves.

RELAXATION

- Simply stand comfortably, arms at your side, and take several deep breaths (wear comfortable, loose-fitting clothing).

- Feel the air as you release each breath. You can close your eyes if you like.

- Breathe at a normal rate and allow your body to relax.

HANG YOUR HEAD

- Let your head hang down forward with your chin touching or nearly touching your chest.

- Drop those shoulders too!

ROLL IT

- Gently and slowly roll your head in a circular motion several times.

- Stop and let your head hang limp again.

- Slowly lift your head up, breathe deeply three or four times, and open your eyes.

FACERCIZE

- Tense the muscles of your head and face. Clench your teeth and tighten your jaw, stretch your cheeks, scrunch your brow.

- Slowly (so you don't hurt your neck) let your head slump down to your chest.

- Sit for a few minutes and enjoy the relaxed feeling.

- Now relax your facial muscles one by one.

STRETCHING OUT

- Sit comfortably, arms at your sides, in a straight-backed chair (you can also lie down) and stretch your legs out in front of you. Keep your legs relaxed.

- Lift your arms slowly and stretch them out in front of you.

TIGHTENING

- Tighten your arm muscles and point your hands straight out.

- Tighten your leg muscles and point your toes straight out.

LETTING GO

- With your arms still tensed and extended, turn your right wrist and hand back and forth as if you were turning a doorknob, trying hard to open a door. Tighten those fingers around the doorknob. Do it several times. (Why won't that door open?)

- Count down from three: three, two one. When you reach one, keep your right arm tense but let your hand drop and your fingers hang limply. Then let your arm drop limply.

- Now do the same with the other hand, fingers, and arm.

GET A LEG UP

- Keeping your right leg tense, lift that leg up slightly and move your foot back and forth several times, as if you were trying to wipe your foot clean on an imaginary wall

- Count down from three: three, two, one. Then let your foot relax, leaving your leg tensed.

- Start bringing your leg down slowly, then let it go limp.

- Now do the same with the other leg.

Relaxing Before You Speak

LETTING GO

An abbreviated version of the above relaxation exercise can work well while you're waiting to go on stage.

- Stand on one leg. Lift the other leg off the ground, bending your knee slightly, and hold the pose for five seconds.

- Shake your leg, shaking out the tension, and then put it down very slowly. Notice that as you put the shaken leg down it feels lighter—this is because of the nervous energy released.

- Do the same with the other leg.

- Stretch out your arms, tensing your arm muscles. Clench your hands into fists.

- Shake out the tension, then slowly bring your arms down to your side.

- Unclench your fists, shake your hands briefly, and wiggle your fingers, then let your arms hang limp.

BASIC DEEP BREATHING RELAXATION EXERCISE

Many athletes and performers use this simple means of breathing properly to relax before a competition. You can use it to reduce stress before you speak, thus allowing you to focus better on the task at hand.

- Preferably standing (but you can do this if you are sitting) with your shoulders straight, take a very deep breath through your nose. Hold it for ten seconds and then release it with force through the mouth. Feel your stomach expand as you inhale and contract as you exhale.

- Repeat three or four times.

PUSHING THAT WALL

You can also release energy by pushing it through the wall. (Note: If you have back or knee problems, this is not for you.)

- Stand with your feet apart about arm's length from a wall and put your hands on the wall. Make sure you are standing firmly and are not on a slippery floor.

- Now push on the wall for a few seconds, bringing one leg forward and bending it as you push your tension through the wall. (Don't do this on anything other than a solid wall. It doesn't work on screens or partitions—believe me!)

- Switch legs and push again.

You can also do this lying down by bending your knees and pushing your feet against the wall. You should be lying firmly on a carpeted floor or else you may send yourself sliding across the floor. One nice thing about lying down and pushing out the tension is that when you are done you can bring your legs up and hug them, knees to chest. This too can feel good.

Visualization

Visualization is a tool that can help you relax almost anywhere. While a quiet room is preferable, you can also practice visualization while waiting on line at the store or even sitting in a traffic jam.

BASIC VISUALIZATION EXERCISE

Picture yourself:

- Walking into a room full of people seated comfortably

- Walking to the stage or the podium

- Looking from the stage or podium out at your audience

- Beginning your speech or presentation

- Seeing the audience sitting quietly and attentively and looking at you as you speak

- Making eye contact with a pleasant face in the crowd, perhaps someone you know

- Concluding your presentation and walking from the stage or podium

- Hearing them applaud

- Feeling a sense of calm at having completed your presentation

(Hint: After you visualize this scene from your perspective on the stage or podium, picture yourself from the perspective of your audience, as though you are watching yourself on tape.)

Add more details each time you do this exercise. For example, add more details about how the room looks, the size of the audience, or any materials you will be using.

Repeating this visualization several times will make the mental experience more comfortable and familiar. This will carry over into your real presentation, keeping you calmer and more relaxed.

SIMPLIFIED VISUALIZATION EXERCISE

In case the previous exercise seems too frightening at first, begin with a simpler version.

- Picture yourself standing up in front of two or three people you feel very comfortable around—friends, your spouse, your children—and telling them what you have to say. Don't present your material—just talk to them. If it's easier, start with all of you seated, then picture yourself standing up as you talk.

- Now add on a few more people that you know. Again, just talk to them. The more you can liken the situation to more casual communication, the less nerve-wracking a speaking engagement will become.

- See them looking at you as you speak. Picture them smiling, even laughing as you make a joke.

- Picture yourself completing what you have to say and sitting down, feeling relaxed and good about having spoken.

POSITIVE VISUALIZATION

A standard and very popular relaxation method, positive visualization
can be done almost anywhere. It
works well if you can let yourself get
lost in your visual imagery.

- Sit comfortably and close your
  eyes.

- Select a peaceful, quiet place such
  as a beach or a park.

- Picture yourself in that place and
  very clearly visualize each of the
  elements around you—sand, grass,
  breeze, scents, and so on. Focus
  on each detail of the setting, letting
  all of your senses take in the
  imagery.

- If you see something that doesn't
  belong, simply take it out of the
  picture.

- After a few minutes, tell yourself
  it's time to leave, and slowly open
  your eyes. Sit for a minute looking
  around. You should feel much more
  relaxed.

Positive visualization has helped
numerous speakers, athletes, and
performers. In fact, some people are
said to be so good at it that they can
visualize themselves on a beach and,
when they're finished, walk away
with a tan.

Planning and Preparation

Planning and preparing for any type of public speaking engagement can make a world of difference. Very few speakers can truly wing it. The better you know your topic and the better prepared you are to present it, the more comfortable you will feel. The fear of making a fool of yourself will greatly diminish as you gain confidence in your ability to present the subject matter. You may even—dare I say it?—come to look forward to your public speaking appearance or engagement.

PLANNING

Architects have blueprints, chefs have recipes, and teachers have lesson plans. Speakers too should have some kind of plan—an outline, an overview, or a summary in whatever form makes you most comfortable.

Presentations will vary greatly depending on the audience, subject matter, and occasion. Someone making a toast at a wedding reception, a person making a presentation in front of the board of directors of a corporation in an effort to procure more funding for a project, and someone conducting an orientation for new college students are going to be taking very different approaches.

Before you begin planning your presentation, you need to ask yourself two questions:

1. Why are you speaking?

2. To whom will you be speaking?

Later we'll look more closely at different types of speaking engagements.

REASONS FOR SPEAKING

So, what is your reason for speaking?

- To persuade

- To inform

- To resolve a problem

- To entertain

- To debate

- To motivate

- To demonstrate

- To honor, pay tribute to, or present an award to someone

- To introduce or welcome someone or something

- To accept an honor or award

GETTING TO KNOW YOUR AUDIENCE

The more you know about the people you will be speaking to, the easier it will be to tailor your presentation. Therefore, you will want to get an idea of who will be in your audience.

For example, a speech at a retirement dinner for a colleague will likely be in front of people who know a great deal about the guest of honor. This allows you to make relatively subtle references to the honoree's habits or traits. On the other hand, at a sales presentation to introduce a brand-new product, you will have to explain the product in detail. Audiences often have a basic level of familiarity with the subject of your presentation but are there to learn new or specific details.

To determine whether you need to start with the basics or can dive right into more advanced details, ask yourself:

• Does your audience know a fair amount about this topic, or is this an introduction to the subject?

• Will your audience be composed of specialists, or will it be a general audience?

To determine their level of interest and enthusiasm ask yourself:

• Are audience members here solely by choice, or were they sent by their employer, for school credit, or for some other reason (such as traffic school)?

• Will they be there for the entire presentation, or will audience members be coming and going throughout the presentation?

To determine the level of language to use and, more importantly, what common reference points to include, ask yourself:

• Is the group of a similar age and similar level of education, or is it very diverse?

• Do audience members have a common interest?

If you are speaking in an effort to persuade others (such as a political speech or rally), ask yourself:

• Is the audience made up primarily of supporters, opponents, or both?

• Is the audience well informed on the topic?

Answers to these questions will help you prepare for your speaking engagement. Do some research on who will be in attendance. If you are in front of an audience and not sure who is sitting out there, you might ask a general question or two in order to determine who is out there and what they know. You might even tell a (tasteful) joke to see how they respond.

REMEMBER, THEY DON'T HAVE TO LOVE YOU

One mistake too many speakers make is trying to please everyone in the audience. The truth is, it simply can't be done. If you speak before a hundred people and one dozes off while two others walk out, you cannot take it personally (unless the two who walk out are your parents).

In most public speaking circumstances, the majority of your audience will be rooting for you to succeed. If not, they're likely to be at worst indifferent. This is not a reflection on you; it may simply mean that people have other things on their minds. For that matter, the person who walks out when you are speaking may have just realized that if he doesn't leave at that moment, he'll miss the last train home. There are many reasons why your audience responds as they do—don't take them to heart.

Part of preparation is telling yourself, "Not everyone will love me . . . and that's okay." Even the finest actors and orators of our time have received bad reviews. It happens!

Some people will not want to like you from the minute you are announced because of the mood they are in on that particular day. Conversely, others may love you not because of anything you've said but because you remind them of someone near and dear to them or because they love your choice of shoes. You cannot possibly address all the reasons why people like or dislike a speaker. The best you can expect from an audience is respect, which means that they remain quiet unless some response is warranted.

Just remember, they don't have to love you!

BECOMING ONE WITH YOUR AUDIENCE

While you cannot be all things to all audience members, you can make some effort to cater to your audience (though the larger the audience, the harder this is to do). Politicians try to do this in overt ways by taking on the look of the crowd in a respectful way (such as by wearing a certain kind of clothing), eating ethnic foods, and so on.

For example, when speaking to young children, the use of exaggerated expressions and gestures can help you hold their attention. Sharing an anecdote that the group specifically relates to can work well. For example, if you're speaking in front of a group of veterans, an anecdote from your days in the military may go over quite well. Speaking in front of college students, you will likely want a more casual approach, while doing the corporate thing calls for an entirely different sort of presentation.

The more you speak in public, the more easily you'll be able to adapt to your surroundings. From your choice of words to your choice of clothes to your body language and gestures, you'll learn to give the people what they want.

PREPARATION MEANS GETTING ORGANIZED

No matter how much research you may need to do, in the end you will want to narrow it all down to 3-by-5 index cards.

First write down your objective—why you are speaking—and prop the card in front of you. In fact, you might keep this on a sticky note.

Next, brainstorm about ideas you could present to your audience, and write each on a separate card. After you have come up with many possible ideas, sort the cards into four piles:

- Ideas you definitely want to talk about

- Ideas you may talk about if you find enough information or have enough time

- Ideas you can eliminate or may use only if trying to stretch

- Ideas you will eliminate

As an alternative, you may use your computer. Create separate files or folders into which you will sort your ideas. (Hint: Print out a hard copy in case disaster strikes your files.)

Once you've sorted your ideas, take the ideas you most want to use and conduct research on each of them. Even if you think you know all about a topic, it can't hurt to look up some of the latest developments or find a recent article from which to quote. Of course, the less you know about a topic, the more you need to do research. Being unprepared makes public speaking infinitely harder. And audiences can usually tell pretty quickly if they know more about the topic than you do.

PRIMARY AND SECONDARY RESEARCH

Primary research refers to data that you generate yourself, through surveys, questionnaires or interviews. *Secondary research* refers to material you gather from books, magazines, newspaper articles, or the Internet. You can use either or both.

SPEECH MAKERS

To make any type of public speaking more informative and enjoyable, you will want to include some of the following elements:

- **Facts and figures.** Make sure they are accurate and current. Double check your sources, especially if they're from the Internet. And unless you're running for political office, try hard not to bend the truth.

- **Quotes.** Make sure quotes are accurate, and attribute them to the correct sources (explaining who they are if they aren't well known). *Bartlett's Familiar Quotations* and other collections of quotations are prime refer-

ences. But don't overdo it—this is, after all, *your* speaking engagement.

- **Stories and anecdotes.** The longer the presentation, the more effective stories or anecdotes will be, since they break up the speech. Keep them concise, and make sure it's clear why you included a particular story or anecdote in your presentation.

- **Examples.** Instead of stories and anecdotes, you may simply cite examples to clarify what you are talking about.

- **Jokes.** Use only humor that's appropriate for your audience— the one about the two nude

sunbathers may not be the joke to tell at a church social. If you're using a joke from a joke book, try to find one that you don't think everyone has heard a million times. If you've written an original joke, try it out on a few people before using it—jokes can be *very* hit-or-miss.

- **Props.** Unless you need a prop for a specific demonstration, use props that are easy to explain and manageable. Also, keep in mind the size of the room. Steve Martin used to get laughs by announcing that he was going to do the disappearing dime trick in a 19,000-person arena.

A BEGINNING, A MIDDLE, AND AN END

It doesn't matter if you're speaking for two minutes or two hours—you need a method to your madness. Make sure your presentation has a specific beginning, middle, and end.

The beginning. Establish your reason for speaking.

- "Tonight I'm going to explain the benefits of the new XL2 super-ultra-micro-mini computer chip, which you can see here on my thumbnail."
- "I'd like to thank everyone for this great honor. . . ."
- "Sales have been down this quarter, and today we're going to address why that is and find out who is responsible."

No, you don't have to state your reason for speaking in the very first sentence. However, somewhere in the early part of your presentation you need to state your purpose. Remember the objective that you wrote down on an index card or sticky note? Incorporate it into a *purpose sentence*—a concise line that introduces why you're speaking.

- "My purpose is to explain the new security procedures that are being put in place around campus."
- "My goal is to welcome new members to our local community organization."

You may have a special opening line that precedes your reason for speaking and grabs the audience. Lou Gehrig began his moving speech upon retiring from baseball with "Today I consider myself the luckiest man in the world."

Opening lines can be very effective. But somewhere early on, you need to make it clear why you are up there.

The middle. This is the meat and potatoes of your presentation, where you present your key points. Here's where you use the facts and figures you dug up with your research to tell them, sell them, teach them, persuade them, dissuade them, or communicate whatever message you have come to deliver. List all the points you want to cover, and make sure to allot enough time for each point.

The end. The longer you talk, the more likely it is that you will need to summarize. Keep in mind that most audience members will remember what you opened and closed with more than anything else. Therefore, make a strong final statement that sums up or enhances your reason for speaking. Many a speaker has saved a mediocre speech with a great final line.

Make sure your audience knows that you're coming to the closing:

- "So, what have we learned here tonight?"
- "In summation . . ."
- "In conclusion . . ."
- "Let me leave you with this thought. . . ."
- "And finally . . ."

Or you may opt for a more entertaining way to signal that your speech is coming to an end:

- "Okay, so you're probably wondering why I've been standing up here rambling for the last half hour."
- "At this point I've completely run out of things to say, so . . ."
- "Before they get the hook and drag me off, remember . . ."

No matter how you do it, plan an ending and try to leave them with something that they'll remember. Don't just talk until someone comes to get you or everyone has left the building.

Practice, Practice, Practice

The only way to improve is to practice. (I've even practiced the outgoing message for my answering machine a couple of times before recording it . . . and I'll bet I'm not alone.) Rehearsing prior to a public speaking appearance will help calm your nerves and build your confidence.

BREATHING PRACTICE

Never thought you'd have to practice breathing, did you? Proper breathing is important for successful public speaking—it helps you pace yourself, it allows you to maintain a steady volume, it prevents you from trailing off at the end of sentences because you are out of breath, and it helps relieve anxiety.

To practice breathing correctly:

1. Stand with your shoulders back (but not too stiff) and your back straight, not leaning to either side.

2. Push your shoulder blades back; this will move your chest forward.

3. Try lifting your chest slightly while keeping your head straight.

4. Let your lower jaw drop naturally while opening your mouth slightly. (Not too wide—you're not at the dentist's office.)

5. Inhale deeply. You want your first breath when speaking to be a good one, so you can begin with a strong voice.

6. Just as you finish inhaling, say, "Good evening. Tonight we're going to talk about several subjects of interest to all of you," as you naturally and slowly exhale. You'll see how the words come out smoothly and clearly as you breathe properly.

IN FRONT OF THE MIRROR

You don't always have to practice in front of the mirror. After all, you won't be looking at yourself when you're on stage. However, the mirror is a way of assessing how you will appear to others as you present your material.

Playing in front of the mirror can help you loosen up and get comfortable with expressions, body movement, and distractions. This will translate into more confidence when you're up there in front of a crowd.

1. Practice the alphabet slowly in front of the mirror. Not that you don't remember it, but you want to become comfortable saying each letter and making each sound clearly. Move those lips.

2. Practice the first three to five lines of your presentation in several different ways.

   - As stone-faced as possible

   - With a cheerful expression and a frivolous manner

   - In an angry or aggressive manner

- While jumping rope, dancing, or moving in any manner

- While impersonating someone you like, saying the lines the way that person would

- While making exaggerated gestures

- Naked (no kidding—one comic said she used to do this)

- With the radio or stereo playing—don't drown yourself out, but give yourself some noise, as there may be some when you are speaking

Try any or all of the above. The point is to become so familiar with the words and the many ways in which they could be presented that you will be very comfortable with what you are going to say. You'll have recited the words in so many different styles that a natural, relaxed tone will come much more easily. You'll be able to say those lines even in the face of distractions. You'll also have some fun with the presentation, making it much more likely that you'll actually enjoy it.

3. Pick the tone that best fits the occasion and practice once more, letting any gestures or movement come naturally. It will be that much easier and probably a lot more fun! Once you've done that, practice again without the mirror.

THE VIDEO CAMERA AND YOU

I once took a communications course where, early in the semester, the teacher had us all get up and give presentations while being filmed. What we didn't know until we watched the tape was that the camera operator had been instructed not to tape us using a traditional shot from the waist up, but to zoom in on fidgeting fingers, tapping feet, hair twirling, and any other typical yet distracting habits. We were all guilty of one or more, and we got a laugh out of the "bad habit" tapes. At the end of the semester, after we'd learned and practiced our speaking techniques, these early tapes provided a sharp contrast in presentation skills.

Practice several times in front of the camera. Have the camera on a tripod, or ask a friend to play cameraperson. Get a full-body shot of yourself, unless you know you will be standing behind a podium. Focus on your words as you speak. Record yourself several times. When watching the tape, look for:

- Fidgeting with your hair or clothes

- Excessive hand movements

- Toe tapping

- Blocking any visuals you may be using

■ Leaning to one side, forward, or backward

■ Rigid body posture

■ Looking off to one side too often

■ Looking down when you talk

■ Slouching, especially if you are seated

■ Touching your clothes, your body, or the microphone

■ Other distracting habits or gestures

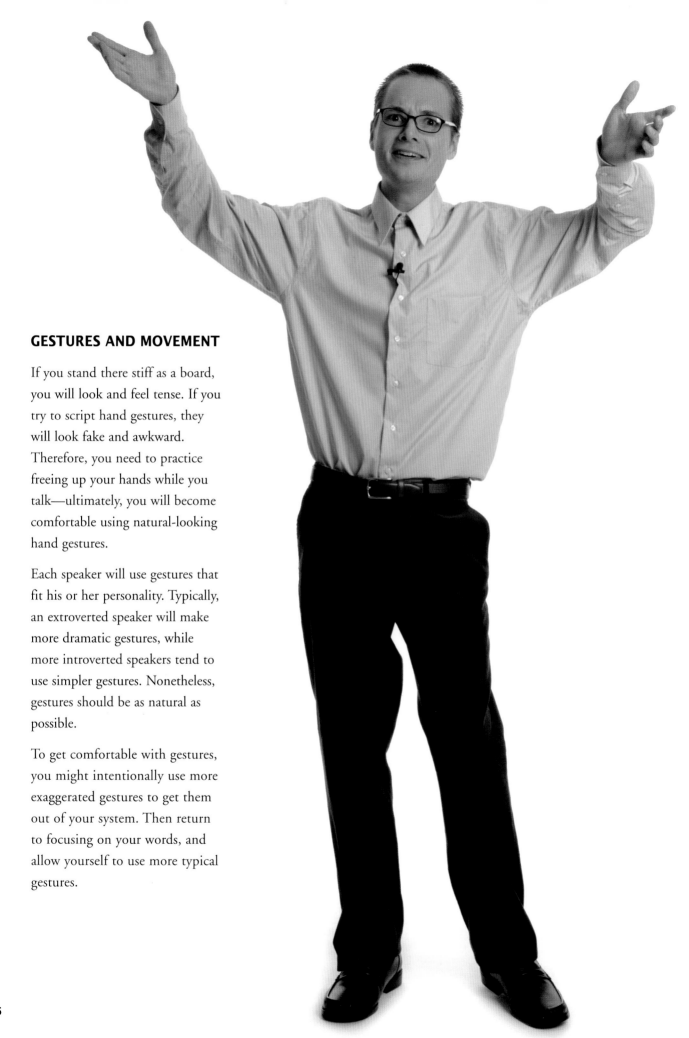

GESTURES AND MOVEMENT

If you stand there stiff as a board, you will look and feel tense. If you try to script hand gestures, they will look fake and awkward. Therefore, you need to practice freeing up your hands while you talk—ultimately, you will become comfortable using natural-looking hand gestures.

Each speaker will use gestures that fit his or her personality. Typically, an extroverted speaker will make more dramatic gestures, while more introverted speakers tend to use simpler gestures. Nonetheless, gestures should be as natural as possible.

To get comfortable with gestures, you might intentionally use more exaggerated gestures to get them out of your system. Then return to focusing on your words, and allow yourself to use more typical gestures.

You can also practice moving around the stage while speaking. Though your movement will be limited by your surroundings, you don't want to appear to be too stiff.

Find a central point on the floor and mark it with a piece of tape. Then practice walking while you talk. Remember not to stray too far from your mark, and keep looking at your audience as you move around.

You'll find more on gestures and movement in the "Fix-Its" chapter.

REHEARSING WITH FRIENDS

After rehearsing a few times on your own, have a good friend or two listen to you speak. Ask your friends to stand in the back of the room; if more than one person is on hand, have them spread out.

After you speak, get some feedback:

- Are you speaking loudly enough?

- Are you speaking clearly?

- Are you doing anything distracting while talking?

- Are you looking down too often?

- Are you talking too quickly or too slowly?

- Are you talking in a monotone?

- Are they getting the general idea of what you're talking about?

- Are your examples clear?

- Do your stories and/or anecdotes help clarify what you're saying?

- Are you asking too many questions?

TIME YOURSELF

Often you will have a limited amount of time in which to speak. Time yourself to make sure you stay within the allotted period (though unless you're speaking on radio or television, where timing is very precise, most speaking engagements can run a couple of minutes long or short without much problem). If you use a watch or stopwatch, try not to look at it once you get started—this is distracting and makes the audience feel that the speaker is anxious to leave. Position your watch, stopwatch, or timer so that you can see it without obviously having to look away.

Even if you don't have a specific time allotment, you should get a general idea of how long you will be speaking. The amount of time appropriate for a presentation will depend on the reason for speaking, the setting, and the number of other speakers.

If you are like me—afraid you'll be looking at your watch constantly— ask someone in the audience to signal you when you have three minutes and then one minute remaining.

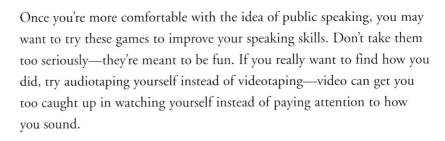

SPEAKING GAMES

Once you're more comfortable with the idea of public speaking, you may want to try these games to improve your speaking skills. Don't take them too seriously—they're meant to be fun. If you really want to find how you did, try audiotaping yourself instead of videotaping—video can get you too caught up in watching yourself instead of paying attention to how you sound.

1. Write down five subjects of interest to you on five pieces of paper. Throw them into a hat and pull one out. Set your alarm clock or a stopwatch for five minutes, stand up and talk on the topic for five minutes straight. Don't worry if you stammer and stumble a bit, it's just a way of getting used to speaking off the cuff.

2. Same as above, except give yourself five minutes to find information and jot down some notes before speaking. While you're speaking, try to refer to the notes as little as possible.

3. With three or more people, have one person select a short pre-pared piece of material such as a magazine article or a passage from a story. Then give the same material to two speakers to study for fifteen minutes. Each speaker will then present the material (notes are allowed, but no copying of the full text). Anyone who's not speaking serves as a judge, deciding who gave the best speech. Use a ten-point scoring system, with 1 to 5 points for knowing the material and 1 to 5 points for presentation.

Suggestions for Instant Public Speaking

Here are some ways you can practice instant public speaking.

- Ask a question at a public event, such as a town council or PTA meeting.

- Make a suggestion or ask a question at a business meeting.

- Give a short presentation in a school. Schools love volunteers, and you can speak about your profession or even read a story to a class.

- Give a short toast at a party.

- Take a class and participate frequently.

- Volunteer at a hospital or similar setting to read to disabled children, to the blind, or to seniors in a group setting.

- Join a school or church choir.

- Call a radio talk show.

Any appropriate situation that affords you a few seconds or a few minutes in front of a group of people can be beneficial, as it gives you a chance to prove to yourself that you can speak in front of others without stress. Look for opportunities in which you are with several other people and can speak up—even telling a story at a dinner party is an example of speaking in front of others. (No, yelling "Surprise!" with forty other people at a party doesn't count.)

Fix-Its

*It seems so easy in front of the mirror, doesn't it?
Of course you're still concerned about the real
thing—speaking in public. So let's see if I can
alleviate some of your concerns by helping you
solve several common problems, starting with the
biggie: stage fright.*

Fear Factor: Stage Fright

Are you ready? It's time to slay the monster. . . .

Stage fright shows up in many forms. For example, you may experience:

- Sweaty palms
- Dry mouth
- Upset stomach
- Shaky knees
- Increased heart rate
- Light-headedness
- Nausea
- An uncontrollable urge to leave the premises

The physical symptoms you experience stem from the emotional fear that you will get up and fail in front of others. This fear can be very great and very real. After all, there are a lot of stress-related what-ifs being tossed around in your mind: "What will people think of me? What if they don't like me? What if I forget what I want to say? What if I'm boring? What if I sound foolish or stupid? Even worse, what if I *look* foolish or stupid? What if they mock me or rebut what I have to say? What if they run screaming from the theater even faster than if the movie *Ishtar* was playing?"

In short, we fear that in the brief moment in time in which we stand before other people, we will be captured in the eyes of the audience on a blooper reel that will last forever.

By this time you're probably ready to pack it in. But don't be so hasty. Stage fright can be overcome.

First, acknowledge your symptoms—dry your hands, take a drink for your dry mouth. Then sit in a comfortable position and focus on your breathing. Use relaxation exercises (as in the previous chapter) to slow a racing heart. Remember, you tense the muscles, then relax them.

The key is not to buy into the physical symptoms and allow them to take over. Remind yourself that these symptoms are not going to stop you from getting up and speaking. They are not going to defeat you.

EASING THE MIND, SLAYING THE BEAST

Here are some tried-and-true ways to combat stage fright:

1. Be very well prepared—and be positively prepared. That means not just knowing your subject matter, but having a positive attitude about your topic. You've got something to say, and you really want to share it!

2. Plan for a nonstressful, relaxing period before you speak. You might even develop a simple pre-speaking routine for yourself, as many performers do.

3. Rehearse several times in conditions that simulate what you'll experience while speaking—with distractions, in front of other people, and so on.

4. If possible, visit the place where you will be speaking. Walk onto the stage; sit in one of the seats and see the stage from the audience's perspective. Get comfortable in the setting.

5. Take a few minutes before you speak to be in a quiet place. Whether it's the green room or the restroom, find a place to do some breathing exercises, visualization, and quiet thinking about your topic.

6. Watch the audience beforehand. You might even want to mingle as they come in, and get to know a few people—if you do, chances are they will be among your biggest supporters. Start liking your audience, and chances are they'll like you!

7. Remember, you do not have to be perfect. In fact, tell yourself you will *not* be perfect. If you make a mistake or something goes wrong, make a joke about it—go with the proverbial flow and use humor as a tension breaker.

8. Avoid stimulants such as coffee or soda with caffeine. Likewise, tranquilizers will give you more than a southern drawl, and alcohol may cause you to give a performance that you may not remember in the morning, and may not want to.

9. Stay in the present. So the piano recital thirty-two years ago didn't go well—you're older and it's in the past. Each speaking engagement stands on its own merits.

10. Remember, 90 percent or more of the people in the audience would be just as nervous as you and would do no better or worse if they traded places with you.

Many speakers and performers put their nervousness to work for them. This means taking that nervous energy and using it to carry you through the speaking engagement.

Jump-starting Your Speech or Presentation

Okay, so you're walking up to the podium or microphone, and you're still nervous. It's time to speak, but nothing is coming out of your mouth. What to do?

- Look around for a friendly or familiar face.

- If there is a podium or place to put your notes, water glass, or anything else you need, arrange those items.

- Take a sip of water to make sure your mouth isn't dry.

- Make a joke about being nervous.

- Stall for a moment by adjusting the microphone slightly, even if it doesn't really need to be adjusted.

- Imagine that you are speaking to one person. One stand-up comic used to name his audience George and imagine he was just having a conversation with George.

Fixing Foul-Ups: Can We Start This Over?

Since one of the biggest fears is that you will screw up, why not prepare for the occasional foul-up? A wrong word or slight flub will probably not even be noticed, so you can just keep on going. Larger flubs require some attention. Johnny Carson, forever the king of late-night talk shows, would have his writers intentionally prepare lines called "savers" that he could use during his monologue when a joke fell flat.

The larger the mistake, the more you need to acknowledge it.

- Immediately tell yourself, "Oops, I messed up. It happens to everyone."

- You might step back from the podium or microphone for a second and regain your composure.

- If you're holding the microphone, you might lower it and take a deep breath, then continue with something like; "As I was trying to say . . ." or "Let's try that again."

- Unless something goes so seriously wrong that you need to stop speaking and call for assistance, you can usually laugh it off or make a joke.

- Sometimes an action will break the tension. Note, however, that if something draws the audience's attention away from you, such as a waiter dropping a tray of drinks at a dinner party, then you need to stop, make a comment, and essentially meet the audience at the point of their attention—in this case the dropped tray—and bring their attention back to you.

Beating the First-Impression Blues

It's a common belief that the first impression you make is critical. And it's true that in the first few seconds, even before you open your mouth, your audience will form an opinion of you, for better or worse. Fairly or unfairly, people rush to judgment.

The reality, however, is that first impressions are somewhat overrated. Many a marvelous presentation has started off slowly and ended with a bang. Nonetheless, it's nice to get off to a good start, if for no other reason than it helps you to relax.

WAYS TO MAKE A BETTER FIRST IMPRESSION

- Calm your nerves by visualizing yourself walking out or getting up to speak shortly before it's your turn.

- Take a quick look in the mirror to make sure your hair, makeup, and clothing are as ready to go as you are.

- Arrive early enough to scope out the room and the audience, and then make an opening comment about something current regarding the group you are speaking to or perhaps about the room where you are speaking.

- Walk in with pride and confidence. Keep your shoulders straight, look at the audience, and smile.

Injecting a little humor into your presentation can relax an audience, brighten up your speech and make it more memorable, and build your confidence . . . if your jokes work. Humor, however, can be a tad tricky. So adhere to the suggested guidelines below:

1. Unless you're doing a comedy routine or a roast, plan to use humor sparingly.

2. Plan humor ahead of time. Even the best comedians are well prepared. This isn't to say you can't ad-lib on occasion, but don't depend on it.

3. Humor needs to fit the crowd. The off-color joke you heard at work is probably not the one to tell in front of the PTA or your church group. Also nix the inside jokes unless you're sure everyone in your audience is an insider.

4. Think reference points. A joke about a typewriter probably won't work in front of a sixth grade class because they may not even know what a typewriter is. Ask yourself, "Will they know what I'm talking about?" Many speakers have bombed using the wrong material for a given crowd.

5. A rule of thumb is that you cannot joke about a minority or ethnic group unless you are part of that group. Even then, make sure you're not stepping over the line of good taste.

6. If you choose to tell a funny story or anecdote, make sure you set the scene clearly. Don't just assume they know the details and jump to a punch line.

7. It helps if you're enjoying the story or the joke you are telling. Smile.

8. Puns and riddles typically do not work.

9. Try to work humor into your speech so that it flows. Don't telegraph an upcoming joke with something like "And now I'd like to tell a joke."

10. Focus on humor that people can relate to from everyday occurrences.

11. Don't be afraid to tell a funny story or joke about yourself. You do not need to be self-deprecating, but it's okay to laugh at yourself.

12. If a joke doesn't get a laugh, just keep on going. You can comment on the joke not working, but never get upset with your audience if they didn't laugh at what you thought was a great line.

Humor is tricky indeed. It is a marvelous way to break the tension, but you still want to maintain your credibility, so you have to know when it fits and when it does not belong. Too many speakers have tried to force a joke in when it isn't the right time or place. Sprinkle humor into your presentation like a chef adding seasoning to a dish.

At a Loss for Words

As you prepare your presentation, you need to think very carefully about the words you will use. Many people have gotten themselves in trouble when failing to select their words carefully—just ask Dan Quayle. Politicians, for that matter, spend an inordinate amount of time correcting and explaining their previous statements.

So how do you choose what to say?

- **Use conversational words.** Whether you are speaking at a formal or informal gathering, you want to speak naturally. For example, "Within the past several days, it has come to our understanding that there has been some discourteous conduct displayed by a portion of our student community" sounds far more awkward than "We have recently learned that some of our students have been behaving poorly."

- **Consider your audience.** Will they understand your choice of words and phrases? An audience of medical practitioners will understand more complex medical terminology than a general audience. Likewise, teens speak their own language.

- **Consider the formality of the gathering.** If people are paying $1,000 a plate for a black-tie dinner, they'll expect higher-priced words.

- **Try to avoid using slang, dude.**

- **Double-check that your wording won't offend anyone.** While you can't guarantee that no one will be offended by what you say, you can try to be politically correct.

- **Make sure that you are consistent.** If you say you didn't have a relationship with an intern in your opening statement, then don't turn around and say you might have had such a relationship a few minutes later.

- **Select words that are inclusive of your audience.** Speeches that have too much emphasis on *I, me,* or *my* can become quite self-indulgent and alienate your audience. Instead you might use phrases like "We can all benefit from . . ." or "You've probably all seen this type of thing before." Even a rhetorical question such as "How many of us really do use deodorant every day?" can hook the audience.

- **To repeat or not to repeat?** It can be awkward if the speaker uses the same word repeatedly for no apparent reason. On the other hand, a catchphrase or buzzword can be effective. You might also repeat a word or a phrase for emphasis. For example: "We need to get involved in our children's education! We need to get involved in local planning issues! We need to get involved in our neighborhood cleanup!"

- **Avoid words you have a hard time pronouncing.** Tape yourself and listen closely. If you find yourself saying "ax" instead of "ask," you need to work on your pronunciation, or find another word.

- **Don't use words you don't understand.**

LOST IN TRANSITION: FINDING YOUR WAY BACK

Ever notice how some speakers can move from one subject to another so smoothly that you didn't even notice the transition? Conversely, you've probably seen speakers who get so lost trying to make a transition that they practically need to send up flares to find the next topic.

Making a smooth transition is a key part of public speaking. Smooth does not always mean unnoticed or subtle. If the audience is taking notes or they are there for the purposes of learning or training, you'll want them to pay careful attention to the fact that you are talking about something new.

Here are some of the ways to make transitions:

- Use a bridge or connecting word or phrase, such as "In addition," "Meanwhile," or "Let's also consider . . ."

- Telegraph points from a list: "Our first topic is . . ." "The second point we want to discuss is . . ." This is not subtle, but it can be very effective when making a presentation or when teaching.

- Insert a short pause.

- Ask a rhetorical question.

- Use movement. You might walk out from behind the podium or sit down on the edge of the desk when starting on a new subject.

- Take a momentary break for questions: "Before I continue, does anyone have any questions?" Note that asking for questions is effective only if you take a couple of questions and save the rest for the end of the talk. Otherwise you'll lose your continuity completely.

Be careful not to use the same transition repeatedly. Some people use the same word, such as *anyway, so,* or *okay,* every time they move on to something else. Awkward repetition gives the impression that you didn't plan very carefully.

Better Posture and Personality

Your energy level and the enthusiasm you have for your topic can be conveyed by the manner in which you are standing. Posture is an important part of the complete communication package that is public speaking.

Shoulders back and chin up indicates confidence and makes it easier for you to project through deep breaths.

Conversely, looking down or slouching gives the impression that you really don't believe in what you're saying.

Sitting can be tricky. Dangling legs look awkward and even childlike, which is adorable if you're five years old but not if you're forty-five. If your feet don't reach the floor from a fully seated position, then perch on the front portion of the seat and put one foot flat on the floor.

In a small, casual gathering you can sit back more comfortably. But always remember to sit up straight. Sit well back in the chair with your feet flat on the floor. Or if it makes you feel more comfortable and will help you avoid the temptation to tap your toes, cross your legs at the ankles. Don't cross your legs higher up—it tends to lead to foot wiggling or playing with shoes or socks.

Note: *Sitting tends to cause people to take shallower breaths and thus to speak more softly. Keep this in mind and don't let it happen to you. Remember to take in a good amount of air and project, even with a microphone.*

Yes, you can rest your hand or arm on a podium, desk, or table, but do it so that you look relaxed and informal while maintaining good posture. Note that leaning does not mean slouching. And don't hang on too tight, or your audience will see that you are nervous.

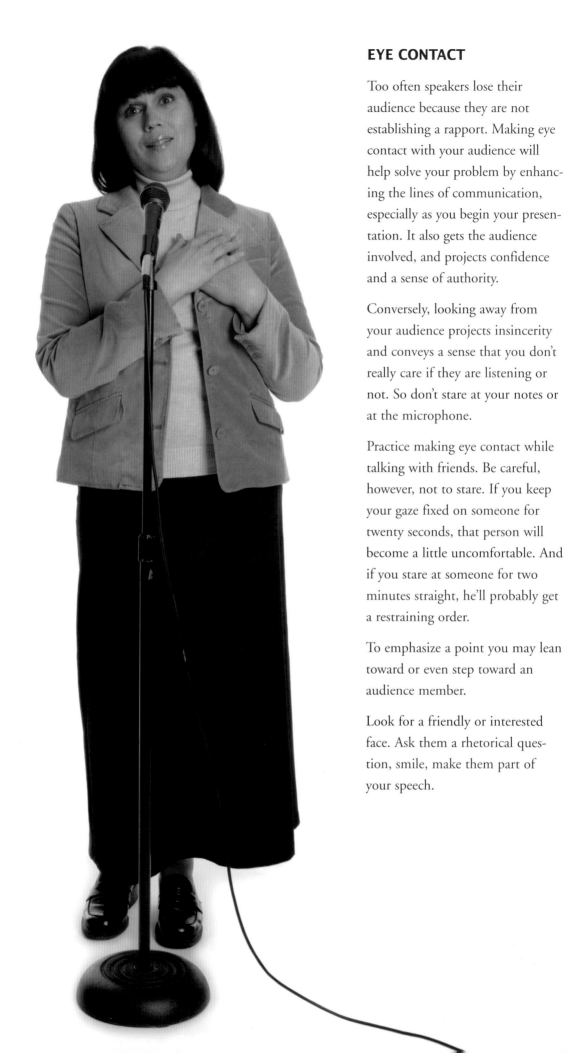

EYE CONTACT

Too often speakers lose their audience because they are not establishing a rapport. Making eye contact with your audience will help solve your problem by enhancing the lines of communication, especially as you begin your presentation. It also gets the audience involved, and projects confidence and a sense of authority.

Conversely, looking away from your audience projects insincerity and conveys a sense that you don't really care if they are listening or not. So don't stare at your notes or at the microphone.

Practice making eye contact while talking with friends. Be careful, however, not to stare. If you keep your gaze fixed on someone for twenty seconds, that person will become a little uncomfortable. And if you stare at someone for two minutes straight, he'll probably get a restraining order.

To emphasize a point you may lean toward or even step toward an audience member.

Look for a friendly or interested face. Ask them a rhetorical question, smile, make them part of your speech.

Note: *The larger the audience or the brighter the spotlight (if there is one), the less likely it is that you will be able to actually make eye contact with audience members. Nonetheless, you want to look at the people you can see. Choose a friendly looking person in the middle of the audience, not in the first row, otherwise the people in the back rows will be look-ing at the top of your head.*

Props: Know When to Hold Them and When to Fold Them

- If your prop is large, such as a flip chart or chalkboard, position yourself to the side and be careful not to block anyone's view.

- Face your audience, not your props. Talk to people, not to objects.

- Reveal your visuals only when you're ready to refer to them.

Props or visuals of any kind can enhance certain presentations and destroy others. If you are doing a corporate presentation, leading a training session, or conducting a demonstration of some type, props—anything from a flip chart to a mockup of a product—may enhance your speech. In the middle of a commencement speech or at a political rally, on the other hand, a prop might seem awkward. Know the crowd and the occasion. Then make sure that whatever you want the audience to focus attention on is being included for a good reason.

- Stop talking when you write on a chalkboard or flip chart. When you're done, turn back to the audience and continue speaking.

- When you're done referring to a visual, turn your flip chart to a blank page to move the attention of the audience back to you while you continue talking.

- Handheld props can sometimes help you illustrate a point. Use them sparingly and hold them at about chest level.

- Depending on the room and the equipment provided, have screens or other major props to the side of the stage, not in the middle. This way you maintain center stage and remain the audience's main focus.

Oh No, I Can't Stop Talking:
The Use of Pauses

Sometimes a two-second pause while speaking in public will seem to last an eternity. Nonetheless, it's worth it if it makes your presentation more effective. Pausing at the right time can:

- Provide your audience with a moment to digest the information (this is particularly helpful when teaching or presenting new information)

- Allow you to catch your breath or to gather your next thought

- Allow you to change topics more easily

- Help you emphasize a point

Comics typically pause before a punch line just momentarily to help emphasize the punch line to follow. Other speakers will pause after a key point in a story to make sure it sinks in. Don't be afraid of the silence.

Now Say It with Feeling

Very often it is not what you say but how you say it that makes the difference between a so-so presentation and a great one. Consider the various ways in which you can say the following sentence and the difference in meaning.

- "I think this presentation will be valuable to everyone in attendance."

- "*I* think this presentation will be valuable to everyone in attendance." The emphasis means the speaker is going out on a limb to imply that this is his or her personal opinion.

- "I *think* this presentation will be valuable to everyone in attendance." The emphasis signifies that the speaker isn't certain about the value of the presentation for the group.

- "I think *this* presentation will be valuable to everyone in attendance." The emphasis states that this specific presentation, as opposed to others, has value.

- "I think this presentation *will* be valuable to everyone in attendance." The emphasis signifies that there has been some doubt about the value of the presentation.

- "I think this presentation will be valuable to *everyone* in attendance." The emphasis implies that some might doubt the value of the presentation to all present.

Clearly, emphasis matters. Emphasize not only with your words but with your expression and your gestures. Make it an entire communication package.

Loosening Up: Adding Some Movement

Are you too stiff on stage? Is someone from the museum building a glass case around you? Then it's time to move!

Movement helps the audience stay attentive while helping you stay relaxed. After all, your muscles start to tense up if you stand in one position for a long time. If you are limited by a lectern or podium, move to the side if possible when you are trying to make an important point.

Always face the audience as you move.

Draw your audience in by coming forward—it makes it seem as though you are talking to them more personally.

Remember to stay centered when moving around—you don't want to give your presentation to only one side of the room.

Note: *Don't overdo it. A little movement can enhance the presentation. Pacing back and forth, however, can become distracting.*

Call to Arms: What to Do with Those Hands and Arms

Many speakers are more comfortable at a podium or lectern because it blocks their lower body and provides a place to rest their hands.

A microphone stand also gives you someplace to put your hands; however, it doesn't look natural or relaxed. If you're not comfortable holding the microphone, place one hand on or behind the stand to keep yourself centered. But leave the other hand free for gesturing. Hold on gently to avoid feedback.

- Hard as it is to do, keeping your arms loosely at your sides makes it easier to gesture and harder to fidget or distract the audience.

- Gently holding your hands in front of you at your waist can be a comfortable alternative and still allow you to make hand gestures as you talk.

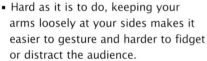

- When you have a wireless microphones or are mikeless, you still need to figure out what to do with those arms. Putting your hands in your pockets makes you look as though you are nervous or trying to hide something.

- The hands-on-hips posture gives the impression that you are either waiting for someone or annoyed.

- Keeping your hands behind your back makes it look like you're either hiding something or ice-skating.

- Crossed arms make you look disinterested—your audience will pick up on this.

- Wringing your hands will make your audience as nervous as you are.

- Some speakers hold a drink or another object. However, if you are going to hold something other than a drink or note cards, chances are it will draw attention, and you will therefore need to mention it.

- Arms hanging straight down can cause you to drop your shoulders. Don't forget to lift your arms to gesture.

- If seated, resting your hands gently on your legs can work.

ALL ABOUT GESTURING

There are four basic types of gestures.

- *Descriptive* gestures help you clarify your words, help create a visual
  image, or define a measurement:
  "It wasn't this big in the catalogue!"

- *Emphatic* gestures emphasize a
  point or a need, such as for unity:
  "To win this election, it is up to you."

- *Suggestive* gestures present a
  thought, idea, or emotion. For
  example, you can easily convey
  that you don't know the answer.

- *Prompting* gestures are used to get
  a specific response from the audience: "Let's hear it for Juan Valdez!"

NOW GET THOSE ARMS AND HANDS WORKING

Let's face it—most of us talk with our hands. Unless you're driving, it helps the communication process. When speaking in public, gestures should be (or at least appear to be) natural and spontaneous.

Gestures should be with the arms away from the body. Arms held too closely to the body will make you appear uncomfortable or robotic.

Be careful not to gesture with the hand holding the microphone.

Note: *Try to avoid using the same gesture over and over again. Repetition can become monotonous.*

It's a Catch-22—you want to practice making unrehearsed, natural gestures, which is, of course, a contradiction. That's why the finest actors make so much money.

Is Your Body Talking Too Much?
Body Language

Have you ever been accused of saying something without even opening your mouth? Sure you have—it happens all the time. From flirtation to fury, body language can speak volumes without the use of any actual words. In fact, studies at the University of California have shown that as much as 55 percent of a speaker's influence comes from his or her body language.

So what exactly is your body saying?

■ This body is saying, "I really wish this was over."

■ This body is saying, "Ask your stupid question."

Last-Second Checklist

Okay, you're about to hit the stage or approach the lectern or podium. Run through this last-minute checklist:

- Check your hair.

- Check your teeth.
- Remember to wear antiperspirant.

- Check your outfit—can you move comfortably?
- Make sure you are wearing no noisy jewelry or other things with which to fidget.
- Have your flip chart, PowerPoint presentation, chalkboard, or other props all set up.

- Make sure you have your notes, and make sure they're in order.
- Did you give whoever will introduce you your introduction?
- Focus on shoulders back, head up, eyes out to audience.
- Remember to breathe as you speak.
- Speak clearly and not too fast.
- Don't forget that pauses are your friends.
- Allow yourself a moment to relax and gather your thoughts.
- Think positively: You can do this—you can wow them!

Many Types of Presentations:

Putting It All Together

In this chapter we look at the specific elements

that make up each of several common types of

public speaking engagements.

The Acceptance Speech

The acceptance speech is a way of saying thank you to those who have honored you in some manner.

Preparation: Prepared remarks should acknowledge those who are responsible for your receiving the honor. Be humble and be gracious, but do not belittle your accomplishments or apologize for them.

If you are one of many people receiving awards, you need to be brief. Create a shortlist of people to thank, and begin thinking of other remarks you want to make. Quoting someone of stature might help you describe your feelings about this accomplishment. You may choose to briefly state what the award means to you or how you got to this point. Time yourself, and trim down such comments by eliminating unnecessary words or lines.

Should you be speaking at a dinner specifically in your honor, you will be expected to speak for a longer period of time, in which case you can tell the story of how your work came to be honored. Again, seek out the highlights and include a pertinent anecdote or two. Speak about what this award means to you, but remember to be humble, and don't use the word *I* ad nauseam: "Then I did this, and then I did that, and I, I, I, I . . ." You may acknowledge others in the audience who have played an instrumental role in your reaching this moment.

If you are being honored or accepting an award, you have done something to reach a certain plateau of excellence or have benefited a business or a community by your work. Whether it's providing a college with the funding for a new gymnasium, topping all widget salespersons in your company for the past year, or devoting hundreds of hours to helping abused and neglected children, you are in a position of respect. Preparing, therefore, means appreciating and passing on the knowledge or experience you have learned or gained.

Tone: Fit the tone and language to the situation. Don't be glib if this is a lifetime achievement award. A joke or two at your own expense is okay. Conversely, you need not make a tear-jerking acceptance speech if you've received a trophy for winning a pie-eating contest. The occasion should warrant an informal conversational tone replete with your own personal sentiment.

Presentation: Your body language should exude pride, not arrogance. Remember, head straight, not in the clouds, and walk with confidence but not with a swagger. Shake hands with or hug whoever is handing you the award, and take a moment to gather your thoughts when approaching the microphone.

Should you be elected or appointed to an esteemed position, whether it is a local political position, president of the PTA, or grand high exalted poobah of your lodge, you'll need to thank those responsible for helping you reach this position, and address what you hope to accomplish while in office.

Be humble, be sincere, talk slowly and with confidence—and try not to make too many promises you can't keep.

The Panelist

If you're asked to speak on a panel, usually the discussion is on a topic with which you are familiar. Panelists generally make statements to present information, join in a general discussion, and/or field questions on the topic.

Preparation: In some cases you will be introduced, and in other situations you may be asked to introduce yourself, meaning you'll provide your name and title or the credentials that landed you on the panel.

If each panelist is afforded a few minutes to speak, prepare your remarks to fit within the given time frame. Notes are always helpful. Tailor your remarks to fit the discussion. Since others will be speaking and may cover some of your intended speech, prepare a couple of alternate routes that you can take so as not to repeat the previous speakers. You should also prepare to answer the most commonly asked questions on the topic.

Tone: A panel discussion usually takes on a professional tone, where you are being called upon to demonstrate expertise in a particular field. Even if you disagree with other panelists you need to allow them the right to present their material or voice their opinions. It's important to be courteous and respectful, unless you're on the *Jerry Springer Show.*

Presentation: Most panels are intended to provide varying views on a topic. You may be one of several people in the same profession providing a specific take on a topic. Listen carefully to what is being said by other panelists and how they respond to questions. Try to present a distinctive voice rather than just reiterating what others have said. Remember that unless the question is directed at you, or unless you have an important point to add, you do not need to answer every question posed to the entire panel. Too many repetitive answers or statements can slow a panel discussion to a crawl.

While you may be addressing the audience, you can refer to what other panelists have previously said by gesturing. Often panelists stay seated and speak. Try to sit up and be the visual focal point of the panel when you are speaking, answering a question, or listening to a statement directed toward you.

Final notes: A good panelist needs to be a good listener, since this is a group setting. Don't dominate the discussion, and don't forget positive body language, even when you are not speaking.

The Toast

The toast is a short ceremonial tribute, a heartfelt moment of celebration and honor. It can be a lyric, a poem, an anecdote, a recounting of some significant moments involving the honoree, or a simple memorable line. It needs only to reflect the moment, the person, the theme, and express sentiment or goodwill.

Preparation: If you know ahead of time that you will be giving the toast, you should write down several key attributes about the person or people being honored. Think of a tasteful, possibly funny story that, in the end, displays a positive attribute of the guest of honor. If you are honoring someone at a tribute dinner, retirement party, or birthday celebration, list several of the person's achievements and accomplishments. Then narrow down your list to those that best exemplify the individual or his or her role on a team. Toasts should be brief and touch the audience in some manner—make them laugh, make them cry, but most of all make them think about the honoree. Remember, it's about the person being honored, not about you.

If you are toasting a couple at a wedding, think of how they met or what they've said about one another. Often a best man or maid of honor will include in the toast a few one-liners about the couple—make them tasteful and don't venture into questionable territory (for example, if you had a fling with the bride, the groom, or both, don't bring it up).

Toasts should be uplifting. They should always end on a sincere note, and you conclude by raising your glasses and taking a drink.

Tone: Cheerful, upbeat and sincere. Display a good feeling about the honoree in your manner, and dress to honor them.

Presentation: The toast is your way of leading a roomful of people in a celebratory moment. You want to use that moment to capture the audience's attention and share it with the honoree(s).

Talk to both the audience and to the honoree. Be eloquent. Don't rush the toast— let your audience have a moment to laugh if you're telling a joke or humorous story. Then pause before the final sincere moment and end with "Here's to . . ." or "Let's drink to . . ." Raise your glass as you finish. Whether you speak for ten seconds or two minutes, make it memorable with the right words and the right sentiment: "Here's looking at you, kid."

Final notes: Toasts are a great way to practice speaking in public because you can do a sincere thirty-second toast and then sit down.

The Sales Pitch: Persuasive Speaking

Paying Tribute

From a retirement party to receiving the Nobel Prize, speeches of tribute or honor are significant milestones for the honoree.

Preparation: First and foremost, know the person being honored. Do some research, talk to other people who know the guest of honor, and build a theme that befits this person. And make sure your facts and stories are accurate! There's nothing worse than talking about the honoree's heroics in World War II only to find out later that he fought in the Korean War.

While you don't want to pour it on to the point where you embarrass the honoree and make the audience queasy, you do want to highlight the accomplishments that have made this person the recipient of this special tribute. Extol the honoree's virtues without overdoing it. Tell stories that demonstrate his or her key attributes, rather than just listing them; mix touching stories with humorous ones and inspiring ones. If you are one of several speakers, you can pick one thing to discuss, such as the honoree's career in business, her love of sports, or her collection of antique dental instruments. Go with a theme. If, however, you are the one and only speaker, try to cover the different sides of the honoree with an emphasis on what he or she is being honored for.

Write material that comes from the heart, and remember as you put your remarks together that this is not about you. In essence, a tribute is an elongated toast.

Presentation: By looking at the audience and at the honoree, through your gestures, and of course through your words, you can reinforce the connection between them, serving as the middle person. Be sincere and deliberate in your manner. Let yourself sound as if you're breaking from your prepared speech to tell a story about the honoree—the story may actually be part of the speech, but it seems more informal if you come out from behind the podium or change your demeanor to a more casual manner, as if to let the audience in on a more personal side of the honoree.

Talk long enough to arouse emotions from the audience but not to the point where you are repeating yourself. Also listen if there are other speakers so you do not repeat their stories about the honoree.

End with "Congratulations," "Best wishes," "God bless," "We're going to miss you," "We all love you," or some such closing statement.

Final notes: Don't overdo it . . . don't underdo it. Often highlighting your relationship with the honoree is the best route to go, since it can include both personal and professional memories.

Mastering the Meeting

Yes, there are one-on-one meetings, but in this case we're referring to meetings with a roomful of attendees—the ones where you'll be speaking in front of a number of other people. Meetings are an excellent place for honing your public speaking abilities, since most of the people on hand are wrapped up in their own personal reasons for being in attendance and wondering when there will be a lunch break.

Preparation: The goal of any meeting is supposed to be to accomplish something, whether it's a new sales strategy for a Fortune 500 company or deciding on how to best run a school bake sale. Therefore, you need to focus first on that goal.

If you are running the meeting, you'll need to prepare an agenda that includes all of the necessary items to be covered that evening. You'll also need to do all the preparations, such as finding and securing a meeting location, making sure there are enough seats,

inviting all necessary attendees (too often people are asked to attend meetings that they have no legitimate reason to be attending), arranging for refreshments, and overseeing all other necessary arrangements. You'll want to plan the seating arrangement to optimize effective communication. For example, a circle might be better than rows of chairs if it's to be a brainstorming session. Additionally, you'll need to script your opening remarks, setting the tone, introducing the subject matter, and explaining what you hope to cover. You'll also want to introduce newcomers and take a moment to hand out any necessary materials. Prepare all of this in advance.

If you are attending a meeting, know why the meeting is being called, and do some research if necessary. Speak up on topics you see in the agenda (which should be distributed in advance) that you have an opinion on or specific ideas about.

Presentation: If you're running the meeting, you want to follow your agenda and try to stick to your timetable. Restate all key points and be as professional as possible, meaning:

• Always be courteous.

• Stay on topic and don't go off on tangents. Also, never gossip about people who aren't there.

• Make sure to speak up, and double-check that the people in the back of a big room or a room with poor acoustics can hear you.

• Look at all attendees as you talk.

• Use movement and gestures to keep it interesting.

• When it's time for others to participate, try hard to include everyone—don't let a few people dominate the meeting. If people are going way off on tangents, look for a way to chime in and reel them back in.

If you are attending a meeting, speak up when called upon or join in when brainstorming. Speak as if you are talking to the person farthest away from you (though you don't need to look at that person); this way you will project. If it will help you be heard, stand up or at least sit up.

While speaking, look at the various people in the room, not just at whomever is leading the meeting or at your boss. You don't want to direct remarks to one person, nor do you want to ignore everyone else. Make concise points, then turn the meeting back over to the leader. Have an end to your comments clearly in sight whenever you start to speak.

Final notes: There are books written about planning and conducting meetings. Participating in a meeting is a great way to build confidence in your public speaking ability. You have the bonus of being completely in control of your time element, meaning you can speak for five minutes or five seconds, depending on what you have to say and your level of comfort. If you're really nervous and just want to get your feet wet, second a motion to vote: "I second that" isn't hard at all.

Up in Front of the Class: The Informative Speech

Technically speaking, you do not need to be in front of a class to teach. There are many situations in which we impart knowledge and provide training. Presenting reports, giving demonstrations, and even running a show-and-tell session are all informative speaking engagements.

Preparation: Unlike a persuasive speech, where you are trying to elicit an action, in the informative speaking situation, you are simply trying to present information in a clear manner that can be understood by your audience. If anything, you are trying to stimulate learning.

As with all other types of presentations, you need to know your audience. In this case, your concern is their level of knowledge and understanding of the subject matter. This will tell you at what level to start. Are you teaching basic math or advanced calculus? An advanced training program will presume a greater level of knowledge about the subject.

Use a variety of reference sources, including books, magazines, the Internet, the media, and interviews, to help you gather your materials. Then develop a logical sequence to explain the information. Use quotes, charts, graphs, surveys, handouts, visuals, or anything else you need to support and enhance your presentation.

Start off simply and gradually move on to more complex materials. Don't assume what the audience knows. Have the backup data available should you need to fill in the blanks or answer any tough questions.

Presentation: Many leading experts know a great deal about their subject of expertise but have a hard time teaching or explaining the material to other people. We've all met very bright people who can't teach. The problem is often that the individual doesn't know how to look at the topic from the perspective of the audience members. You've probably come across someone who knows the ins and outs of computers but can't help you repair yours because he or she is speaking in computerese and you're not fluent in that high-tech language.

It helps to present information in increments, modules, or sections, which explains why lesson plans are divided up into discrete parts. It allows the audience to digest information in comfortable doses. The more complicated the material for a specific audience, the more you will need to slow down, pause, reiterate, and take breaks.

A good teacher knows how to read the faces and expressions of his or her students. When trying to inform, you need to have a sense of how much information is getting from your mouth into the minds of those listening. You need to know when they've stopped listening.

Final notes: Talk to your audience before launching into the material. If you can establish a rapport, it becomes easier to teach. Answer questions that are general in scope and save more specific or detailed questions for after the class, session, or demonstration.

Mastering Television

Congratulations, you've made the big time. Television is a powerful medium. You need to be very well prepared and well rehearsed if you're going to make a good impression. After all, the camera doesn't lie.

Preparation: First, you want to dress correctly. The camera can add several pounds, so avoid the doughnuts in the green room before going on, and if you have slenderizing clothes, wear them. You also don't want to wear complicated patterns or bright colors that will distract the audience. Solid colors and pastels work well. Don't wear anything that will reflect the bright lights, including shiny jewelry. While you want to look good, you also want to dress in a manner that is camera-friendly.

Watch the program you will appear on in advance. Get a feel for the tone of the show. Unless you are in an acting role with a prepared script, you will likely be there to answer questions in an interview. In some cases you will be able to suggest the questions, and in most cases you will know what you will be asked to talk about.

Prepare short answers that are conversational, informative and entertaining. Practice in advance so that you articulate your answers clearly. Also practice sitting up or standing in a comfortable position with your shoulders back yet not too stiff.

Presentation: Limit hand gestures, since they may not be on camera, but don't forget facial expressions, as they may be accentuated through close-ups.

Make eye contact with the interviewer as you respond, but don't stare. Keep your body and head also facing the camera. Hint: Be aware which camera is on—note the red light on top. If you are speaking directly into a camera (for example, taping a public service announcement or making a charity drive appeal), look at the camera as if you were talking to another person.

Be careful not to focus on your image on the monitors; your eyes need to be on the camera. Keep your eyes relaxed—don't stare, and don't squint even if the lights are bright.

Since the camera can get closer to you than your typical audience, touching your face or fidgeting in any manner can be that much more obvious. Be conscious of positive body language. Remember that you will breathe better and speak better if you are sitting up.

While it is not your responsibility to make sure the show is running on schedule, you may need to be aware of time cues.

If you are on television for promotional reasons, make sure to present your message clearly, and reiterate where and when your audience can buy it, sell it, or see it.

Should you be presenting information, which could include giving a demonstration, be personable, upbeat, and confident in what you are teaching or explaining. Unless it is your show, you'll need to talk to both the host and the camera.

Also remember that entertainment value is part of the lure of television, even on informational and educational programming.

Final notes: Don't play with the microphone. Don't fidget. Don't swivel in the chair if you are seated. Don't use words that cannot be said on network television. Wear makeup—that goes for both men and women. Also, make sure you hair is just as you would like it to be right before airtime. Ask for help with hair and makeup.

You've Got the Perfect Look for Radio

Unless your shirt is so loud that it's coming over the airwaves, your look and your gestures are not factored into your radio appearance. However, every little um, ah, or unnecessary noise may sound like a ton of bricks falling.

Preparation: In many ways, speaking on the radio isn't like public speaking because you are not speaking in front of the public—well, not obviously. The act of sitting behind a microphone in a small studio and talking is far less intimidating than staring out at an audience seated before you or even into a camera lens. However, the reality is that you may be heard by a very large audience, many of whom are ready to hit the button on the dashboard if you are boring.

To prepare for radio, you need to write out your presentation and practice until you are smooth.

While you can read from a prepared script, unless you're reading news or advertising copy you'll want to have a more natural, conversational manner. Therefore, you'll want to paraphrase your own words or speak from notes or index cards.

If you're in a group setting, you want to avoid talking over others. Signaling is allowed. Typically, the stream-of-consciousness talk radio persona is the end result of a lot of preparation and experience in the medium. Even shock jock Howard Stern does plenty of preparation for a show and works closely with his staff.

Use audiotapes to listen to yourself and see if you can eliminate unnecessary utterances between key words or phrases. Also try to be aware of words you use over and over, and cut them way back. You should do this before any type of public speaking, but especially for radio, where all you've got to work for you is your voice . . . and the occasional sound effect.

Work on pronunciation and correct word choice: it's *ask,* not *ax; hundred,* not *hunred; nuclear,* not *nuculer; regardless,* not *irregardless.*

Presentation: The sound technician will be responsible for getting the right level for your microphone. Arrive early enough to get used to talking and hearing yourself while wearing a headset.

Be aware of the time factor. Like television, radio typically works on a tight time schedule. However, unlike television, you can look at the clock or your watch often.

Keep in mind that while no one can see if you slouch, it can affect how much energy you have when you speak. Therefore, you might sit up for better breathing.

Since you can't rely on your good looks and pearly white teeth, you'll have to sound intelligent, entertaining, amusing, controversial, and/or engaging to keep 'em listening. Whether you like him or hate him, Howard Stern is a master at holding listeners' attention by building on a theme, no matter how crude, and always leading listeners to believe something more outrageous is coming up next. The more engaging you are, the more they'll want to keep listening.

Final notes: Avoid dead air—keep on talking. Be aware of cues to go to a commercial break or at the end of the program. If you are reading scripted copy, practice it several times and underline words or phrases that you need to emphasize.

MANY TYPES OF PRESENTATIONS

When They Call On You: Impromptu Speaking

At a meeting, in a class, or perhaps at a seminar, you may be called upon to speak on the fly. Sometimes impromptu speaking is a blessing in disguise, as you have no time to build up stress and worry. Other times it can be a disaster if you're not paying attention. Remember the teacher who called on you when you were trying to nap in math class?

Preparation: The best preparation for impromptu speaking in a group setting, such as a meeting or classroom, is to be a good listener. Follow the discussion and formulate ideas and opinions just in case you're called upon.

If you are asked to step up and speak on a topic or fill in for someone who is absent, you'll want to take the first few moments to stall while gathering your thoughts. Thanking the audience for coming and letting them know how pleased you are to be speaking are simple ways of stalling while you decide what to say.

Don't apologize and tell them you're not prepared. Understand that the audience does not expect you to produce something like Martin Luther King Jr.'s "I have a dream" speech. They simply expect you to do your best under the circumstances.

Use your few seconds of preparation (or stalling) to think of three key points on the topic. Then think about why the audience is here and see if you can meet their needs in some manner. Do they want to learn something? Are they here to be motivated? Are you at a sci-fi convention where you can make stuff up and they're likely to buy it if you can sound like Rod Serling?

One way in which you might structure an impromptu speech is to use a chronological approach to talk about the subject, such as:

- When you started at the company
- The present state of the company
- Where you see the company going in the future
- Ideas you have for change or progress

Presentation: If you weren't supposed to speak, then no one will be expecting anything from you. Therefore, the pressure is off.

Take a deep breath, speak slowly and deliberately, and focus attention on being enthusiastic and upbeat. You'd be surprised at the minimal amount of substance you need if you are truly likable. While you may not want to say it aloud, keep telling yourself, "They like me—they really like me."

It is most imperative in these circumstances that you rise to the occasion by telling yourself not to panic. In some cases, if you just relax and let your thoughts unwind, you can actually get on a roll and talk for several minutes on a subject almost by rote. You may even find that you did well up there but can't remember what the heck you said. Impromptu speaking can be exhilarating.

Final notes: Remember, it's okay to be vulnerable. If you start struggling or fumbling, laugh or make a joke or comment about being tongue-tied. Audiences are very forgiving.

High Drama: Onstage Performances

"The show must go on!" "Break a leg!" "Where's my contact lens?"

Yes, you'll hear many clichés prior to a performance, but your focus needs to be on giving the audience 100 percent. Whether it's a solo performance at Carnegie Hall or a local community theater production, performers need to work long and hard on preparation before getting in front of an audience.

Preparation: Being prepared and well rehearsed is the professional approach. Study your lines, rehearse on your instrument, or go through the dance routine until you have perfected it. Whatever you will be doing onstage needs to be rehearsed to the point where it becomes second nature. This will allow you to be in the moment, to connect with the audience, and make any adjustments if necessary.

In most situations, you'll do the same performance whether 25 or 25,000 people are sitting in the audience, so you need not assess the crowd. Comedy, a magic show, or perhaps an afternoon presentation of a play for children may need to be altered to fit the audience.

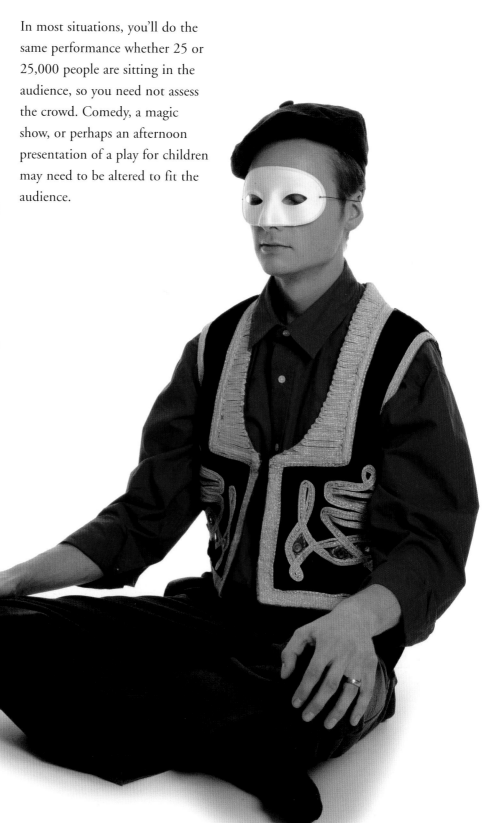

With a day job in public relations and formal training as a classical singer, **Holly Teichholtz** has spent enough time on stages of one sort or another to feel comfortable speaking in public. In fact, there have probably been times when her friends and family wish she were somewhat less okay with it.

Animals and children fall madly in love with **Gina Vetro**, who acts, plays classical piano, and is not afraid of crowds. She lives with her two dogs, Mrs. Peeps and George Clooney.

Scott Vinnacombe is an aspiring film actor with plenty of theater and public speaking experience under his belt. Too lazy to deal with regular "everyday" jobs, Scott is always happy to spend his time posing as a wimp.

Adrienne Truscott speaks in public all the time.

Matthew Wittmeyer is a photographer who lives in New York City with his wife, a third-grade teacher. He is quite comfortable with public speaking, because it pales in comparison to his next project: becoming a dad.

Index

A

Acceptance speeches, 96–97
Anecdotes, 38
Arms. See Hands/arms
Attitude
    Changing, 14
    Toward audience, 35, 36
Audience
    Attention of, 14–15
    Attitude toward, 35, 36
    Eye contact with, 19, 76–77
    Getting to know, 34
    Keeping them awake, 92
    Questions from, 90
    Targeting, 36
    Word selection for, 70

B

Beginning, of presentation, 39
Body language, 88–89
Breathing, 19, 40–41
Breathing exercises, 27–29
    Basic deep breathing relaxation, 27
    Pushing wall, 28–29

C

Carson, Johnny, 57
Classroom speeches, 112
Clip-on microphones, 63
Clothing, 66–67, 114
Computer, 37
Confidence, preparation and, 18

D

Descriptive gestures, 86
Dressing for success, 66–67, 114

E

Emphasis, 81
Emphatic gestures, 86
End, of presentation, 39
Energy
    Keeping them awake, 92
    Posture and, 74–75
    Relaxation and. See Relaxation;
        Relaxation exercises
Examples, 38
Exercises. See Breathing exercises; Practice;
        Relaxation exercises; Visualization
Eye contact, 19, 76–77

F

Facercize, 24
Facts and figures, 38
Fear(s). See also Fix-Its; Nervousness
    Affirmation against, 19
    Conquering, 17, 18–19
    Of making mistakes, 14
    Stage fright, 54–55
First impression, 58–59
Fix-Its. See also Gestures/movement;
        Hands/arms
    Answering questions, 90
    Appropriate humor, 38, 68–69
    Body language, 88–89
    Checklist, 93
    Dressing for success, 66–67, 114
    Eye contact, 19, 76–77
    First-impression blues, 58–59
    Fixing foul-ups, 57
    Introductions, 91
    Jump-starting presentations, 56
    Keeping them awake, 92
    Memory mending, 60–61
    Microphone management, 62–65
    Moving around stage, 47, 82–83

Pauses, 80
Posture, 74–75
Props, 38, 78–79
Stage fright, 54–55
Word emphasis, 81
Word selection, 70–73
Friends, rehearsing with, 48

G

Games, speaking, 50
Gestures/movement, 46–47. See also
        Hands/arms
    Basic types, 86
    Body language and, 88–89
    Moving around stage, 47, 82–83
    Natural, 46, 87
Get a leg up, 25
Getting started, 16–19

H

Habits, identifying bad, 44–45. See also
        Fix-Its; Mistakes
Hands/arms, 84–87. See also
        Gestures/movement
    Microphone use and, 64, 84–85
    Natural gestures with, 46, 87
    While seated, 85
Hang your head, 23
Head relaxation exercises, 23
Humor
    Appropriate, 38, 68–69
    Jokes, 38, 56, 59, 69, 103
    Roasts, 102–103

I

Ideas, organizing, 37
Impromptu speaking, 118–119

Inclusive words, 71

Index cards, 37

Informative speeches, 112

Insecurities, 14

Instant public speaking, 51

Introductions, 91

J

Jokes, 38, 56, 59, 69, 103

Jump-starting presentation, 56

K

Key, to public speaking, 14, 18

L

Lecterns. See Podiums

Length, of presentation, 49

Letting go, 25, 26

Loosening up (movement), 47, 82–83

M

Master of ceremonies (MC), 104–105

Meeting presentations, 110–111

Memorizing material, 60–61

Microphones, 62–65

    Audience questions and, 90

    Clip-on, 63

    Common mistakes, 64–65

    Hand use and, 64, 84–85

    Mastering, 62–63

    Wireless, 85

Middle, of presentation, 39

Mind-set, changing, 14

Mirror, practicing with, 42–43

Mistakes

    Fixing, 57. See also Fix-Its

Identifying bad habits, 44–45

    Moving through, 19

Movement. See Gestures/movement

N

Nakedness, 18

Nervousness, 12–15

    Changing attitude toward, 14

    Channeling nervous energy, 15

    Eliminating, 19. See also Fix-Its

    Insecurity and, 14

    Stage fright, 54–55

O

Onstage performances, 120–121

Organizing, 37

P

Panelist appearances, 98

Pauses, 80

Paying tribute, 109

Perfection, 19

Persuasive presentations, 100–101

Planning/preparation, 19, 32–39

    Acceptance speeches, 96

    For audience, 34–36

    Benefits of, 14, 18, 32

    Classroom speeches, 112

    Confidence and, 18

    Impromptu speaking, 119

    Informative speeches, 112

    As key to speaking, 14, 18

    Master of ceremonies presentations, 104–105

    Meeting presentations, 110

    Onstage performances, 120–121

    Organizing and, 37

Panelist appearances, 98

For paying tribute, 109

Persuasive presentations, 101

Planning overview, 32–33

Presentation parts, 39

Radio presentations, 116

Reasons for speaking, 33

Rebuttals/responses, 106

Roasts, 103

Sales pitches, 101

Targeting audience, 36

Television presentations, 114–115

Toasts, 99

Welcoming speeches, 108

Podiums

    Arranging materials on, 56

    Moving around, 47, 82–83

    Posture at, 75

    Security from, 84

Political correctness, 70

Positive visualization, 31

Posture, 74–75

Practice, 18–19, 40–50

    Benefits of, 18

    Breathing, 40–41

    Daily interactions as, 123

    Feedback and, 44–45, 48

    With friends, 48

    In front of mirror, 42–43

    Gestures/movement, 46–47

    Identifying bad habits, 44–45

    Instant public speaking, 51

    Locations, 19

    Speaking games, 50

    Timing yourself, 49

    With video camera, 44–45

    Where to start, 19

Presentation

    Beginning, 39

    End, 39

Introductions, 91
Jump-starting, 56
Middle, 39
Speech makers, 38
Transitions, 72–73
Word selection for. See Word selection
Presentation types
Acceptance speeches, 96–97
Classroom speeches, 112
Impromptu speaking, 118–119
Master of ceremonies, 104–105
Meetings, 110–111
Onstage performances, 120–121
Panelists, 98
Paying tribute, 109
Persuasive presentations, 100–101
Radio, 116
Rebuttals/responses, 106–107
Roasts, 102–103
Sales pitches, 100–101
Television, 114–115
Toasts, 99
Welcoming speeches, 108
Primary research, 38
Prompting gestures, 86
Pronunciation, 71
Props, 38, 78–79
Positioning, 78
Revealing, 78
Using appropriately, 79

Q

Questions, handling, 90
Quotes, 38

R

Radio presentations, 116
Reasons for speaking, 33

Rebuttals, 106–107
Rehearsing. See Practice
Relaxation, 18, 19
Relaxation exercises
Basic, 22–26
Facercize, 24
Get a leg up, 25
Hanging head, 23
Letting go, 25, 26
Rolling head, 23
Stretching out, 24
Tightening, 24
Research
Organizing, 37
Primary, 38
Secondary, 38
Responses, 106–107
Roasts, 102–103

S

Sales pitches, 100–101
Seated presentations
Hand use and, 85
Microphone use and, 63
Posture, 75
Secondary research, 38
Speaking games, 50
Speech. See Presentation
Speech makers, 38
Stage fright, 54–55
Starting speaking, 16–19
Stories, 38
Stretching out, 24
Success. See also Fix-Its
Last-second checklist, 93
Speech elements for, 38
Summary points, 123
Ten tips for, 19
Suggestive gestures, 86

T

Television presentations, 114–115
Tightening, 24
Timing yourself, 49
Toasts, 99
Tone
Acceptance speeches, 96
Master of ceremonies presentations, 105
Panelist appearances, 98
Toasts, 99
Topics, organizing, 37
Transitions, 72–73

V

Visualization, 30–31
Basic exercise, 30
Positive, 31
Simplified exercise, 30
Visuals. See Props
Vulnerability, 19

W

Welcoming speeches, 108
Wireless microphones, 85
Word selection, 70–73
Audience and, 70
Consistency in, 71
Emphasis and, 81
Formality of event and, 70
Politically correct, 70
Pronunciation and, 71
Transitions and, 72–73
Using conversational words, 70
Using inclusive words, 71